Deciding to apply to the Peace Corps takes research and deliberation. This catalog is a great resource as you explore opportunities to serve as a Peace Corps Volunteer.

What's Inside?

Peace Corps Mission 2

Peace Corps Overview 3

A Living Legacy for Today's World 4

The Volunteer Experience 5-7

Benefits During Service 8

Benefits After Service 9-10

What the Peace Corps is Looking
for in a Volunteer Applicant 11-13

What Makes a Successful Volunteer? 14-15

Core Expectations for Volunteers 15

Understanding Selection and Placement 16-17

The Application Process 18-19

Map of Where
Peace Corps Volunteers Go 20-21

Job Descriptions and Qualifications 22-36

Tear-out Application Process Tipsheet 39

Want to jump ahead?

Look for answers to these frequently asked questions:

What is Peace Corps in a nutshell? 3

How long is the program? 5

What kind of training is provided? 5

What is the work schedule? 5

What are living accommodations like? 5

Will I be the only Volunteer
in my community? 5

How can I stay in touch while I am abroad? 6

What if I get sick or injured? 6

What about my health and safety? 6-7

What about family emergencies? 7

Can family and friends visit me? 8

Do I have to pay anything? 8

What will I be paid? 8

What if I have student loans? 8

Am I allowed vacation time? 8

What are the benefits of volunteering? 8-10

What if I'm considering graduate school? 8,10

What support is available upon returning? 9-10

Who may apply? 11

What if I don't have a college degree? 11

What educational background is required? 11

Do I have to know a foreign language? 11

Is there an age limit? 13

Can couples serve together? 13

What if I have an existing medical issue? 13

How do you decide where I will go
and what I will do? 16

What is the application process? 18-19

What kind of work will I be doing? 22-23

Learn what Peace Corps service is really like on the ground, around the world

For over 50 years, the Peace Corps has remained true to its service mission, established in 1961.

Mission of the Peace Corps

The Peace Corps promotes world peace and friendship by:

- Helping the people of interested countries in meeting their need for trained men and women
- Helping promote a better understanding of Americans on the part of the peoples served
- Helping promote a better understanding of other peoples on the part of Americans

Friend Us, Fan Us, Follow Us

Stay in touch through Peace Corps social media.

Facebook: facebook.com/peacecorps

Twitter: twitter.com/peacecorps

YouTube: youtube.com/peacecorps

Flickr: flickr.com/peacecorps

Tumblr: peacecorps.tumblr.com

LinkedIn: linkedin.com/company/peace-corps

Peace Corps Digital Library: peacecorps.gov/collection

Peace Corps Positions Overseas

Annually, more than 8,000 Volunteers and trainees are in the field.* They work in the following program areas:

●	Education	36%
●	Health and HIV/AIDS	22%
●	Business and Information & Communication Technology	15%
●	Environment	14%
●	Youth Development	5%
●	Agriculture	4%
●	Other**	4%

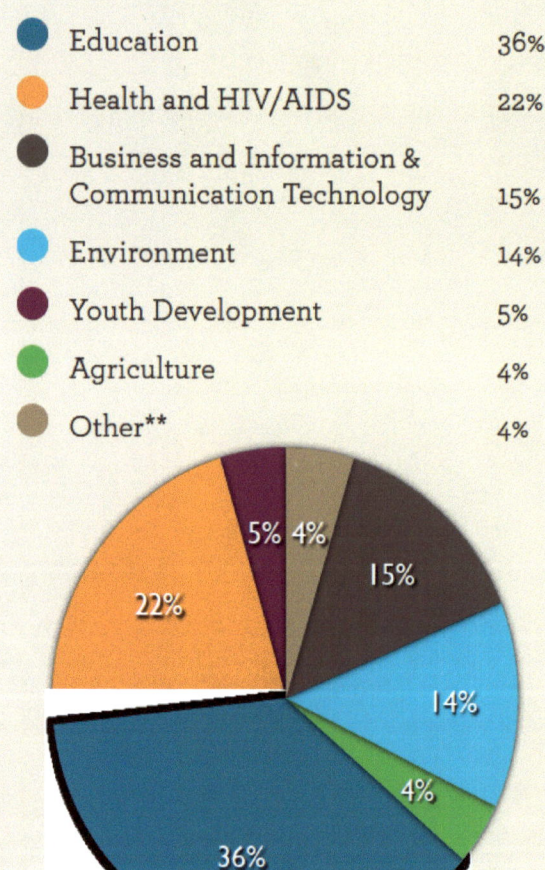

*Data average of past two years
**Other category includes Peace Corps Response Volunteers and Volunteers working across sectors

*Find informational meetings in your area, interact with recruiters through virtual webcasts, or review recruitment presentations at **peacecorps.gov/events**.*

Peace Corps Overview

The Peace Corps provides Volunteers to more than 70 countries requesting assistance in Africa, Asia, the Caribbean, Central America and Mexico, South America, Europe, the Pacific Islands, and the Middle East. The Peace Corps is an independent U.S. government agency.

Thousands of new Volunteers are needed each year to work in a variety of areas, including:

- Education
- Health and HIV/AIDS
- Business and Information & Communication Technology
- Environment
- Youth and Community Development
- Agriculture

The length of service is 27 months, which includes an average of three months of in-country training that provides language, cross-cultural, technical, and health and safety skills.

Volunteers are placed where their skills match the needs of host countries. They live in the communities they serve, from small rural villages to large urban cities. Their work around the globe represents a legacy of service that has become a significant part of America's history and positive image abroad. Their desire to make a difference has improved the lives of millions of people around the world and at home.

Volunteers return to the United States as global citizens, with leadership, cross-cultural understanding, and language and technical skills that position them well for professional opportunities.

The Peace Corps is a life-defining leadership opportunity and a great way to launch a career.

Unlike many other international volunteer programs, there is no fee to participate in the Peace Corps.

To be eligible for service, you must be:

- At least 18 years old
- A U.S. citizen

Volunteers have a variety of skills, work experience, and education levels—90 percent have at least an undergraduate degree. There is no upper age limit. The average age of Volunteers is 28. Currently, the oldest Volunteer is over 80.

The benefits of being a Volunteer are many, including the following Peace Corps provisions:

- Student loan assistance
- A "readjustment" allowance of $7,425 (pre-tax) upon completion of service
- Language, cross-cultural, and technical training
- Travel to and from country of service
- A monthly living and housing allowance
- Medical and dental care
- 48 paid vacation days
- Leave for family emergencies
- Graduate school opportunities such as scholarships, credit for service, fellowships, and internships
- Transition and job support and social networking after service
- Advantages in federal employment

The Peace Corps recommends that you submit your application as early as possible so we can match your skills to openings as they become available. Plan ahead and apply nine months to a year in advance of your desired date of departure.

A Living Legacy for Today's World

The Peace Corps traces its roots and mission to 1960, when then-Sen. John F. Kennedy challenged students at the University of Michigan to serve their country in the cause of peace by living and working in developing countries. From that inspiration grew a federal government agency devoted to world peace and friendship.

Throughout its history, the Peace Corps has adapted and responded to the issues of the times. In an ever-changing world, Peace Corps Volunteers have met new challenges with innovation, creativity, determination, and compassion. From AIDS education to emerging technologies to environmental preservation to new market economies, Peace Corps Volunteers have helped people build better lives for themselves. Their work in villages, towns, and cities around the globe represents a legacy of service that has become a significant part of America's history and positive image abroad.

Reflecting the Faces of America

Since 1961, more than 200,000 Volunteers have served with the Peace Corps to promote a better understanding between Americans and the people of 139 countries. This unique heritage continues to inspire Americans to make a difference every day.

One of the goals of the Peace Corps is to help the people of other countries gain a better understanding of Americans and our multicultural society. The agency actively recruits people with a variety of backgrounds and experiences to best share our nation's greatest resource—its people—with the communities where Volunteers serve around the globe.

Learn more at
peacecorps.gov/whovolunteers.

"Peace Corps is a special job. There is an emphasis on development, but a focus on understanding the people with whom we are living. It is when people know us and trust us that we are able to be our most effective."

Chris Morrill
Volunteer in El Salvador and Bolivia

"Peace Corps Volunteers live in and become members of the communities they serve. It's much easier to exchange information and raise awareness on issues, and it shows that Volunteers care about a community's problems and would like to help solve them."

RuKan Takidakashu
Host country counterpart in Ukraine

The Volunteer Experience

Period of Commitment

Peace Corps Volunteers serve 27 months, generally spending three months in training and 24 months on the job. Each Volunteer serves in a single community in one of more than 70 countries, assisting in a needed area as specified by each host country. There may be just one Volunteer in a particular community, with the closest Volunteer being hours or days away, or there may be several Volunteers in the same city.

Peace Corps Training

Training begins in the U.S. prior to departure. Then the Peace Corps provides two to three months of training in the country in which Volunteers are assigned to serve. Volunteers study together and receive intensive instruction in the local language, usually from native speakers. They also learn technical skills related to their jobs and become familiar with the country's cultural traditions. During this period, most Volunteers live with host families to fully immerse themselves in the new culture. At the completion of training, Volunteers possess the language, technical, and cross-cultural skills needed to begin their work and are then sent to their individual sites. Over the next 24 months of service, the Peace Corps provides Volunteers with regular opportunities to reinforce existing skills and gain new skills related to work, language, culture, and safety.

Work Schedule

Volunteers work with counterparts and/or local government or nongovernmental organizations. This facilitates the Volunteer becoming part of the community he or she serves. The work Volunteers perform is important, but so is the experience of living in another country and interacting with its people. The length and structure of a Volunteer's workday depend on the particular job, and there are opportunities to build friendships and develop additional projects in conjunction with one's community.

Living Conditions

Peace Corps covers the cost of housing and other necessities. Volunteers live in both rural and urban communities. Housing accommodations vary greatly, from a simple hut to an urban apartment, but all must meet the Peace Corps' standards for safety and suitability. There may or may not be electricity or running water. Facilities may be as basic as a squat toilet. Some Volunteers share housing with a local family or a co-worker in their assigned communities, while others live by themselves.

Site selection is based on many criteria, such as site history; access to medical care, banking, postal, and other essential services; access to communication, transportation, and local markets; availability of adequate housing and living arrangements; and agreements with host country authorities and communities.

Communication While Abroad

Most Volunteers are able to maintain contact with friends, family, and fellow Volunteers by text messages, email, phone, or mail. Over 90 percent of Volunteers have a cellphone. Access to these modes of communication can vary greatly from site to site—some with limited technology. In all cases, the Peace Corps has systems in place to contact each Volunteer should there be a family emergency or an emergency in-country.

Peace Corps Support Abroad

In each country where Volunteers serve, there is a Peace Corps office and staff, managed by a country director (one office serves several islands in the Eastern Caribbean). Members of the staff include a safety and security coordinator, medical personnel, program managers, and trainers. Medical staff members provide Volunteers with the basic medical skills and supplies needed to stay healthy. They provide primary care as needed and visit Volunteers at their sites periodically over the course of their service. If a health problem occurs that cannot be treated locally, the Peace Corps, at its own expense, will send the Volunteer to an appropriate facility in a nearby country or back to the United States.

Volunteers work with counterparts and/or local government or nongovernmental organizations, arranged by Peace Corps. This facilitates the Volunteer becoming part of the community he or she serves.

If you decide the Peace Corps is not right for you at this time, there are other volunteer opportunities. For more information, visit **peacecorps.gov/alternatives.**

Family Emergencies

If a death occurs in a Volunteer's immediate family, the Peace Corps allows a leave period and pays for the Volunteer's travel home. Immediate family is defined as a parent, spouse, sibling, child, or grandchild related to the Volunteer by blood, marriage, or adoption. This includes step-relatives (e.g., stepmother), but does not include in-laws (e.g., mother-in-law).

Volunteer Safety and Security

The health and safety of Volunteers is the Peace Corps' highest priority. The agency devotes significant resources to provide Volunteers with the training, support, and information they need to stay healthy and safe.

Yet because Volunteers serve worldwide, sometimes in very remote areas, health and safety risks are inherent. Peace Corps is committed to protect Volunteers and provide effective support. Each Volunteer receives guidance during training concerning locally appropriate behavior, exercising sound judgment, and abiding by Peace Corps policies and procedures.

To ensure a productive, healthy, and safe experience, the Peace Corps evaluates work and housing sites in advance, and collaborates on project development with local communities. In choosing sites to place Volunteers, the Peace Corps carefully considers factors such as access to medical and other essential services and availability of communications and transportation, particularly in cases of emergency.

The Peace Corps has a country-specific emergency action plan in place for which each Volunteer is trained to address such events as natural disasters or civil unrest. The plan ensures Volunteers can be contacted in case of an emergency and for important notices. In a crisis, the Peace Corps coordinates with the U.S. Embassy in each host country to share information, develop strategies, and coordinate communications.

Visit peacecorps.gov/safety
to learn more.

Benefits During Service

Pay and Living Expenses

The Peace Corps provides Volunteers with a living allowance that enables one to live in a manner similar to the local people in his or her community, covering housing, food, and incidentals. It provides complete dental and medical care during service, including shots, vaccinations, and medicines. It also covers the cost of transportation to and from the country of service. Unlike other international volunteer programs, there is not a fee to participate in the Peace Corps.

Deferment and Cancellation of Student Loans

Volunteers with Perkins loans may be eligible for a partial cancellation benefit. School loan deferments exist for several federal programs (i.e., Stafford, Perkins, direct, and consolidated loans). Some commercial loans may also be deferred during Peace Corps service. Because the rules that authorize deferment are complicated and subject to change, it is best to talk to your lending institution about how this benefit applies to your particular situation.

Vacation Time and Visits

Volunteers receive two vacation days per month of service—a total of 48 days over two years. Many use this time to travel to nearby countries. Some invite family or friends to visit so they can share their experience of the host country. And, of course, Volunteers can use this time for a visit home (at their own expense).

Combine Graduate School and Peace Corps

If the idea of the Peace Corps interests you, but you want to go to graduate school soon, you can do both with Master's International. At more than 80 campuses nationwide, Master's International offers 100+ programs in a wide range of fields. Begin your studies on campus, serve overseas with the Peace Corps for two years, then return to school to finish your graduate work. As part of your service, you'll work on projects related to your master's studies. You'll return to campus with practical knowledge in your field, a wealth of incredible memories, and enough significant international experience to land the right job. A list of participating schools and fields of study can be found at **peacecorps.gov/masters**.

Benefits After Service

Develop Skills for the Global Marketplace

Fluency in foreign languages, international experience, and cross-cultural understanding are highly sought-after assets in today's global economy. The Peace Corps provides you with up to three months of intensive training before service begins and offers continued training throughout your service. Whether you are just out of college, mid-career, or retired, the new skills you learn can help you achieve long-term career goals by enhancing your marketability to employers. Volunteers returning from abroad have used their Peace Corps experience as the foundation for successful careers in a variety of areas, from government to business to education.

Earn Funds for Transition

The Peace Corps recognizes that returning from overseas requires some adjustment, so when you complete your 27 months of service, it provides $7,425 (pre-tax) to help with the transition to life back home. This money is yours to use as you wish.

Extend Health Benefits

Take advantage of affordable health insurance for up to 18 months following Volunteer service. The Peace Corps pays the first month's premium and you then have the option to purchase a reasonably priced insurance policy to cover you and qualified dependents.

Lifetime Eligibility for Graduate School Financial Benefits

Returned Volunteers are offered reduced tuition, assistantships, and stipends at more than 60 participating campuses in a variety of subject areas through the Paul D. Coverdell Fellows Program. Fellows combine graduate study with substantive, degree-related internships that help meet the needs of underserved American communities. A list of participating schools and fields of study can be found at **peacecorps.gov/fellows**.

Receive Advantages in Federal Employment

Volunteers who complete two years of service receive one year of noncompetitive eligibility for employment in the federal government. This means that at the hiring agency's discretion, if a Volunteer meets the minimum qualifications for a position, he or she can be hired without going through the standard competitive process. Those who are employed by the federal government after their Peace Corps service can receive credit toward retirement for those years of Volunteer service.

Career Support After Service

When Volunteers return to the U.S., Peace Corps Returned Volunteer Services (RVS) provides transition assistance related to jobs and education. RVS publishes online job announcements, graduate school information, and career-related articles and advice; sponsors career events throughout the year in Washington, D.C., and other cities; and helps returned Volunteers translate their field experience for prospective employers and other professional contacts.

Employment Opportunities at Peace Corps Partner Organizations

The Peace Corps has partnerships with other federal agencies, international and domestic nongovernmental organizations, volunteering and service organizations, minority higher education institutions, and other domestic nonprofits. Your Peace Corps service strengthens your competitiveness for employment with Peace Corps partner organizations. These nonprofit, government, and community development organizations are eager to apply your overseas experience to programs at home and abroad. Visit **peacecorps.gov/careerpartners** for a list of partner organizations.

Be Part of a Vibrant Network

Extend your Volunteer experience by being part of the more than 200,000 returned Volunteers, many of whom actively participate in local returned Peace Corps Volunteer (RPCV) groups.

Unique Opportunity for Short-Term Assignments

Peace Corps Response is a program that offers short-term, high-impact assignments overseas for returned Volunteers and other experienced professionals. Positions average six months in length and are designed to address development needs as identified by the host country. There are a small number of assignments, selection is competitive, and requirements are different than for a Peace Corps Volunteer. Visit **peacecorps.gov/response** for more information.

What the Peace Corps is Looking For in a Volunteer Applicant

What Can Help Any Applicant

Although their specific duties and responsibilities vary widely, Peace Corps Volunteers serve in the following areas: Education, Health, Business Development and Information and Communications Technology, Environment, Youth and Community Development, and Agriculture.

Education: Highly competitive candidates have a college degree in agriculture, forestry, or environment, paired with Spanish or French language skills. Ninety percent of Volunteer positions require a bachelor's degree. Competitive non-degree candidates can qualify for agriculture and forestry extension with more than one year of full-time work experience in agriculture or environment. The Peace Corps also considers work, hobbies, and volunteer experiences that align with the skills it is seeking.

The Peace Corps is partnering with minority education institutions to increase access to higher education. Visit **peacecorps.gov/higheredpartners** for a list of higher education partners.

Language: There is no second language requirement to serve as a Peace Corps Volunteer; however, some regions, including Central and South America and parts of Africa, require Volunteers to know Spanish or French prior to arrival. To minimally qualify, candidates should have at least two semesters of Spanish or French at the university level or have completed four years of a romance language in high school within the last eight years. If you have learned a language informally, the Peace Corps may consider CLEP and ACTFL exam results for placement. Applicants are encouraged to build upon their existing foreign language skills through coursework or self-study.

Leadership and Community Service: The Peace Corps seeks applicants with leadership skills and community service. Leadership in your community, school, faith-based group, or service organization – particularly in planning activities, organizing, and motivating groups of people, and project supervision – will strengthen your application. Qualifying volunteer experiences are supervised, structured assignments that meet specific community needs with expected outcomes.

Visit **peacecorps.gov/volunteerpartners** for volunteering and service opportunities that can strengthen your Peace Corps application and prepare you to support community projects around the world.

Professional Skills and Experience: Demonstrating motivation and commitment, work skills and knowledge, social sensitivity, and emotional maturity will help any applicant. Establishing a good track record of employment and successfully achieving job competence may help demonstrate your productivity.

Flexibility: The more flexible you are in terms of your Peace Corps geographic location, your assignment area, and your desired departure date, the greater your chance of being nominated and possibly invited to serve as a Peace Corps Volunteer. Your flexibility allows placement staff to find the most appropriate matches for your skills and education.

To be considered for Volunteer service you must be at least 18 years old and a U.S. citizen.

How to Become a More Competitive Applicant

Want to be a competitive candidate for Peace Corps service? If you do not have a specialized degree as outlined on pages 22-36, you may qualify with a bachelor's degree in any discipline paired with the experience listed below:

Agriculture 3-6 months of full-time experience with a large-scale commercial or family-run business involving vegetable gardening, farming, nursery work, tree planting and care, urban forestry, livestock care or management, or fisheries work.

English Teaching 3-6 months of English or foreign language tutoring in a structured program that provides training. Your student(s) must be at least 12 years old, and you must complete at least 10 hours of tutoring each month. Many opportunities in this area do not require a foreign language. All education positions require a minimum GPA of 2.5.

Health Extension 3-6 months of volunteer work experience in health education, specifically educating youth, high-risk groups, peers, or the general public in healthy lifestyle promotion and/or disease prevention. The most in-demand experience is with HIV/AIDS, family planning, and nutrition. Public health departments and local community health organizations are the best resources for finding volunteer opportunities.

> *Talk to your recruiter about how to be a more competitive applicant.*

If you have these skills, you are very competitive for Peace Corps service

The following skill sets are highly sought by our host countries:

- *Agriculture economics with or without a foreign language*
- *Forestry with French*
- *Environment with Spanish*
- *Agriculture with Spanish or French*
- *TEFL/TESL with classroom teaching*
- *Teaching credential (BA/BS)*

A Variety of Skills and Backgrounds Needed

Reflecting the diversity of America: The Peace Corps actively recruits people with a variety of backgrounds and experiences to best share our nation's greatest resource—its people—with the communities where Volunteers serve around the globe. The Peace Corps welcomes people from every background and does not discriminate against anyone based upon race, color, religion, sex, national origin, age (40 or over), disability, sexual orientation, gender identity, gender expression, marital status, parental status, political affiliation, union membership, genetic information, or prior participation in protected activity including grievance proceedings.

Those in mid-career: Peace Corps can enhance an existing career or launch a new one. International leadership experience can lead to many opportunities upon return to the U.S. Many returned Volunteers begin new careers based on their work experience in the Peace Corps.

There is no upper age limit for Volunteers: Older applicants have a wealth of life skills, professional experience, and tested maturity to offer the Peace Corps. Seven percent of current Volunteers are age 50 or older, and this segment continues to grow. When deciding to apply to serve in the Peace Corps, many older Americans have questions about issues unique to this stage of life, such as insurance, Social Security, maintaining home and financial affairs while overseas, etc. Recruiters can provide more information. Also, visit **peacecorps.gov/50plus**.

Couples: The Peace Corps will make an effort to place couples who are married, but please be aware that the opportunities to place couples are more limited than those for individual applicants. Both you and your spouse must apply at the same time and qualify for assignments in the same country. Couples who have been married for at least a year before they begin service have traditionally been better able to adapt to the challenges of the Peace Corps than those who are newly married.

In Good Health: Due to the nature of countries where Peace Corps serves and the scope of the medical services available in each of those countries, all applicants undergo a comprehensive medical and dental assessment based on their health history and examinations to determine if they are medically qualified to serve in the Peace Corps. A list of conditions the Peace Corps is typically unable to support can be viewed at **peacecorps.gov/medical** and is also available from your recruiter.

What Makes A Successful Volunteer?

Flexibility: As a Peace Corps Volunteer, you will likely be placed in an environment very different than anything you've experienced in the United States. Letting go of expectations and being flexible will assist you in handling whatever comes your way. For example, Volunteers live like the neighbors they serve, so there may be varying levels of access to running water, electricity, or other resources. Housing is safe but may be basic. Also, in many countries, the way you dress is seen as an expression of respect. To be accepted, you may have to conform to the standards in your host country and community.

Adaptability: Having the ability to adjust to the many new and different situations you encounter as a Peace Corps Volunteer allows you to be responsive to the people you will live with and serve. You may appear as outlandish to your new community as your new life is to you, and you will need to adapt to a much less private existence than you probably had back home. Sometimes it may seem like you're living in a fishbowl.

*Visit **peacecorps.gov/game** to test your skills in a fun simulation of Peace Corps work.*

Responsibility: As a Peace Corps Volunteer, you are a vital part of a larger team assigned to your country of service. Peace Corps' highest priority is the safety and security of its Volunteers and has policies in place to mitigate risk. For example, while a Volunteer, you will not be able to drive a vehicle, nor leave your community without notifying Peace Corps staff.

Sense of Humor: Having the ability to laugh at yourself and at life's little surprises goes a long way. Your service will be a continual learning process. Keeping a lighthearted view will help you learn from your mistakes without judging yourself harshly. Besides, laughter is universal.

Patience: This is not a job for people seeking quick fixes or instant gratification. Instead, you will need to work creatively to develop relationships with community members, and to build trust and motivate various stakeholders. This all takes time.

Skill: Being selected as a Peace Corps Volunteer means you have the technical experience and education needed by a host country. The Peace Corps will additionally prepare you by providing language, cross-cultural, and project-specific training. Continuing to hone these skills during your service will enable you to make a meaningful contribution to the community you serve.

Self-Reliance: Although you may feel like you are never alone as a Volunteer, you may also feel very "on your own." You are likely to be the only Peace Corps Volunteer in your community. You will face language barriers and the challenge of finding your way around a new neighborhood. You can expect to be well-received by the community, but initially you will be dealing with things as simple as learning people's names. Having a strong sense of self-reliance will help you navigate moments of doubt and challenging situations.

Positive Attitude: The structure of your job assignment and the work itself will probably be less defined than what you have experienced in the U.S. There may be times when the work flow feels chaotic or times when it is slow. A positive attitude can ease the transition.

Resourcefulness: As people adjust to new environments and cultures, they go through certain predictable emotional states: loneliness and isolation, insecurity and uncertainty, homesickness, and doubts about their commitment to serve. By being resourceful, working with what you have, and keeping an open mind, you will be able to overcome these challenges and thrive.

Core Expectations for Peace Corps Volunteers

In working toward fulfilling the Peace Corps mission of promoting world peace and friendship, as a trainee and Volunteer, you are expected to:

1. Prepare your personal and professional life to make a commitment to serve abroad for a full term of 27 months.

2. Commit to improving the quality of life of the people with whom you live and work; and, in doing so, share your skills, adapt them, and learn new skills as needed.

3. Serve where the Peace Corps asks you to go, under conditions of hardship, if necessary, and with the flexibility needed for effective service.

4. Recognize that your successful and sustainable development work is based on the local trust and confidence you build by living in, and respectfully integrating yourself into, your host community and culture.

5. Recognize that you are responsible 24 hours a day, 7 days a week for your personal conduct and professional performance.

6. Engage with host country partners in a spirit of cooperation, mutual learning, and respect.

7. Work within the rules and regulations of the Peace Corps and the local and national laws of the country where you serve.

8. Exercise judgment and personal responsibility to protect your health, safety, and well-being and that of others.

9. Recognize that you will be perceived, in your host country and community, as a representative of the people, cultures, values, and traditions of the United States of America.

10. Represent responsibly the people, cultures, values, and traditions of your host country and community to people in the United States both during and following your service.

How Peace Corps Determines Selection and Placement of Volunteers

How and where the Peace Corps assigns Volunteers to work is based largely on:

- How well your skills match the open positions we have
- How your skills compare to those of other candidates
- Your availability and suitability, and the start date of open positions
- What support is available should you have special medical requirements

The more flexible you are about where you serve, the easier you are to place.

Each year, Peace Corps places thousands of Volunteers in positions that have been created in collaboration with the countries requesting assistance. The start dates for these positions depend on the country and the job.

In a year, Peace Corps receives many applications. Some applicants are not qualified enough to proceed to nomination. Some are not competitive enough to receive an invitation. Some people withdraw from the process. Recruiters interview and evaluate candidates who may qualify based on skills and suitability. The recruiters then nominate candidates for general work categories in regions of the world and forward the candidates' information to Peace Corps headquarters for legal clearance, placement consideration, and final medical evaluation and clearance.

The medical evaluation plays a part in both qualification for service and country assignment, taking into consideration any medical support that may be necessary. For a list of conditions the Peace Corps is typically unable to support, visit **peacecorps.gov/medical** or ask your recruiter for a copy.

Following legal clearance, the names of those candidates who are nominated and successfully complete an initial medical review are forwarded to a placement officer. Placement officers conduct a suitability review, considering motivation, commitment, productivity, emotional maturity, and social sensitivity. A placement officer may also contact you with additional questions. He or she will compare your skills to those of other candidates, review the timing of your availability and current job openings, and consider any medical support necessary. At this point, some nominated candidates will be evaluated as noncompetitive or not suitable for service. Placement officers determine final matches and issue invitations. The specific job and country offered may be different than those initially recommended by the recruiter, resulting from the variables mentioned. After invitations are accepted, candidates complete a final medical evaluation before departure for service.

1. Requests by countries to fill jobs

2. Candidates submit Volunteer application and Health History Form

3. Recruiter search and review of candidates

4. Candidates nominated by recruiters

5. Legal clearance

6. Placement suitability evaluation and matching for different categories of jobs and many departure dates

7. Invitations sent to selected candidates

8. Invitees make acceptance decision

9. Final medical evaluation

10. Invitees become trainees and depart for their country assignments

The Application Process

On average, the application to invitation departure process is seven to 12 months, but may take longer in certain cases. This is due to a number of factors, including the number of positions available, turnaround time for reference checks and the medical evaluation, and determination of applicant suitability for assignments.

Step One: Application

The first step toward becoming a Peace Corps Volunteer is to start your application. You can do this by going to **peacecorps.gov/apply**. The application does not need to be completed in a single session. You will use your email address and create a password for your application so you can work on it periodically. You will need to access your application at least once every 30 days in order to keep it active. Most people complete the application within two weeks. During this stage you will submit all of the following items:

- A completed application form, which includes two essays, three references, employment history, resume, a list of community and volunteer activities, educational background, and practical skills information

- A copy of your college transcripts unless, generally, you have 10 years applicable professional experience (an unofficial copy of an official transcript is acceptable)

- Outstanding student loan, mortgage, or other financial obligation information

- Documentation on outstanding legal obligations

- A completed Health History Form

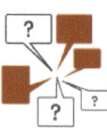

Step Two: Interview

You will be contacted after an initial review of your application—usually within two weeks. For applicants deemed potentially qualified, an interview generally takes place after all application materials, including references, have been submitted. During the interview, you and the recruiter will discuss your skills and interests, job opportunities available, and your personal attributes, such as flexibility, adaptability, social and cultural awareness, motivation, and commitment to Peace Corps service. This is an opportunity to ask questions and explore with the recruiter—who is almost always a returned Volunteer—if the Peace Corps is appropriate for you and how you might best fit our job openings.

Step Three: Nomination

After the interview is complete the recruiter will evaluate your candidacy. If the recruiter determines you are qualified for Peace Corps service and there are open positions, you will be nominated to serve in a general work area and region of the world with an approximate departure date. Based on your responses on the Health History Form, you may need to provide additional medical information before you can be nominated for a specific program. A nomination is a recommendation for an applicant to move to the next stage of consideration, which includes legal clearance, suitability, technical skills review, and final medical clearance. After you are nominated you will be mailed fingerprint cards and a National Agency Checklist form. These must be completed and returned to the Peace Corps before the next steps of the process can begin.

Step Four: Medical, Legal, Suitability, and Competitive Reviews

After being nominated, your application will also be reviewed for eligibility based on the Peace Corps' legal guidelines. This is a review of documentation you provided related to marital status, financial obligations, previous arrests and convictions, dependents, etc.

Applicants who are medically pre-qualified and legally cleared for Peace Corps service are then evaluated by a Peace Corps placement officer for suitability and compared to other candidates based on skills. A placement officer may contact you for follow-up information. Competitive and suitable candidates will then be matched to openings, taking into account your available departure date and availability of medical support, should you have any special requirements.

Step Five: Invitation

For qualified and competitive candidates, the placement officer will extend an invitation in writing for a specific country and provide a detailed job description. The electronic invitation letter includes the date of departure, the program job assignment, and links to a welcome packet with details about the country where you will serve (the Welcome Book), a Volunteer Handbook, and more.

If you accept the invitation to serve as a Volunteer, the Peace Corps will send you more information about your host country, and provide information on your pre-service orientation training and departure.

Step Six: Final Medical Clearance

After you accept your invitation, and 60 days prior to your departure, you will be required to complete a physical and dental examination. At the minimum, the physical examination includes a trip to your doctor for a medical exam with lab work, some immunizations, and a visit to your dentist for X-rays. The Peace Corps offers some limited cost-sharing reimbursement according to a fee schedule. Depending on whether you have insurance, some costs incurred during this process will be at your expense. All materials requested from the medical staff should be returned no later than 30 days after your physical and dental examinations. The majority of applicants are medically cleared for Peace Corps service; some require placement where additional medical support can be provided; and some cannot be placed. Visit **peacecorps.gov/medical** for information on conditions that the Peace Corps is typically unable to support, or ask a recruiter for a list.

Step Seven: Preparation for Departure

The Peace Corps travel office will issue an electronic ticket for travel to your pre-service orientation site (also known as staging). Immediately prior to leaving for the country of assignment, Peace Corps "trainees" meet in the U.S. to prepare for their Volunteer service. You will meet others in the training group and, a short time later, fly to your assigned country to begin in-country training.

Use the Tipsheet on the following page to track your application process.

Where Volunteers Serve

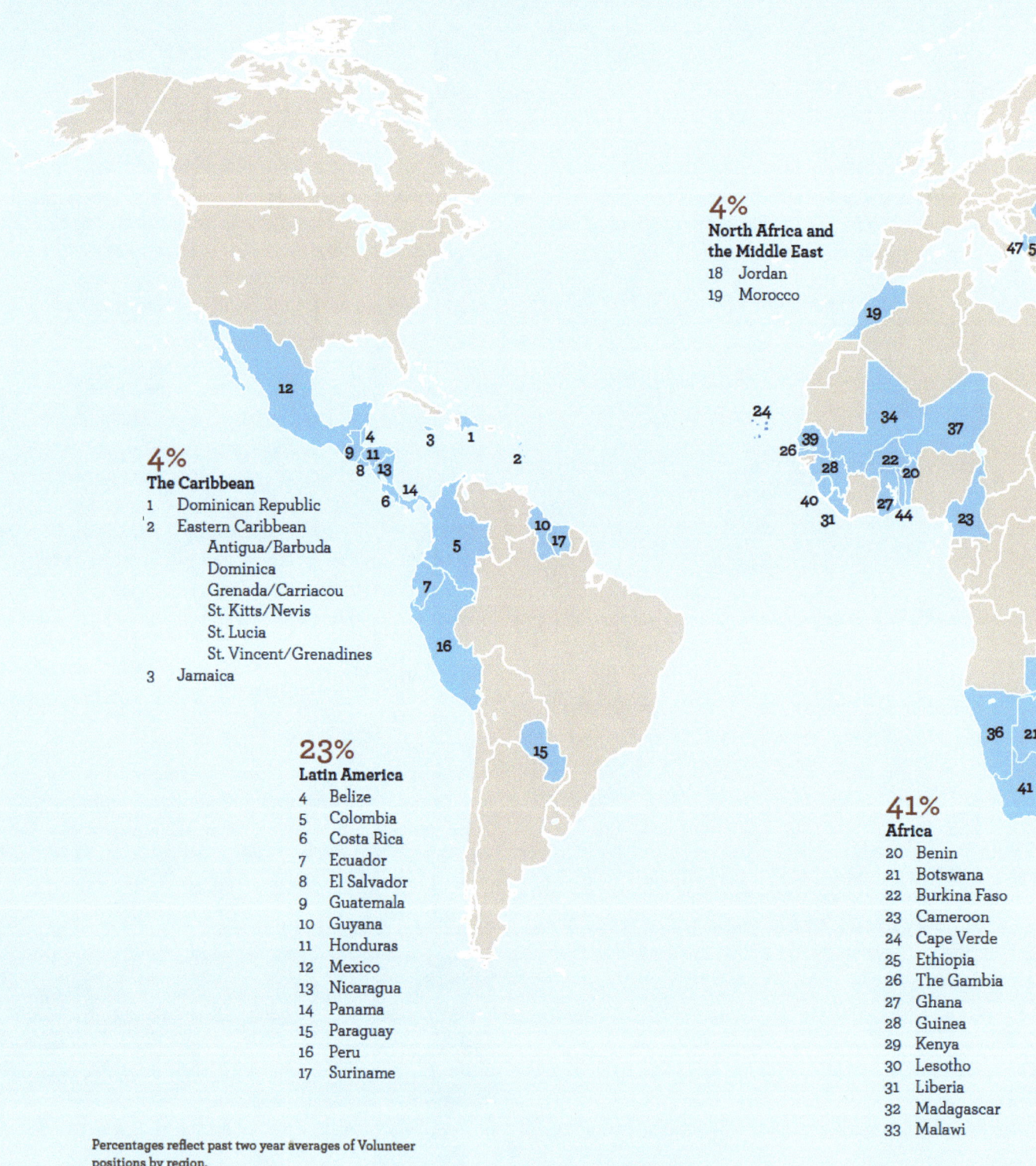

4%
North Africa and the Middle East
18 Jordan
19 Morocco

4%
The Caribbean
1 Dominican Republic
2 Eastern Caribbean
   Antigua/Barbuda
   Dominica
   Grenada/Carriacou
   St. Kitts/Nevis
   St. Lucia
   St. Vincent/Grenadines
3 Jamaica

23%
Latin America
4 Belize
5 Colombia
6 Costa Rica
7 Ecuador
8 El Salvador
9 Guatemala
10 Guyana
11 Honduras
12 Mexico
13 Nicaragua
14 Panama
15 Paraguay
16 Peru
17 Suriname

41%
Africa
20 Benin
21 Botswana
22 Burkina Faso
23 Cameroon
24 Cape Verde
25 Ethiopia
26 The Gambia
27 Ghana
28 Guinea
29 Kenya
30 Lesotho
31 Liberia
32 Madagascar
33 Malawi

Percentages reflect past two year averages of Volunteer positions by region.

Countries as of September 2011

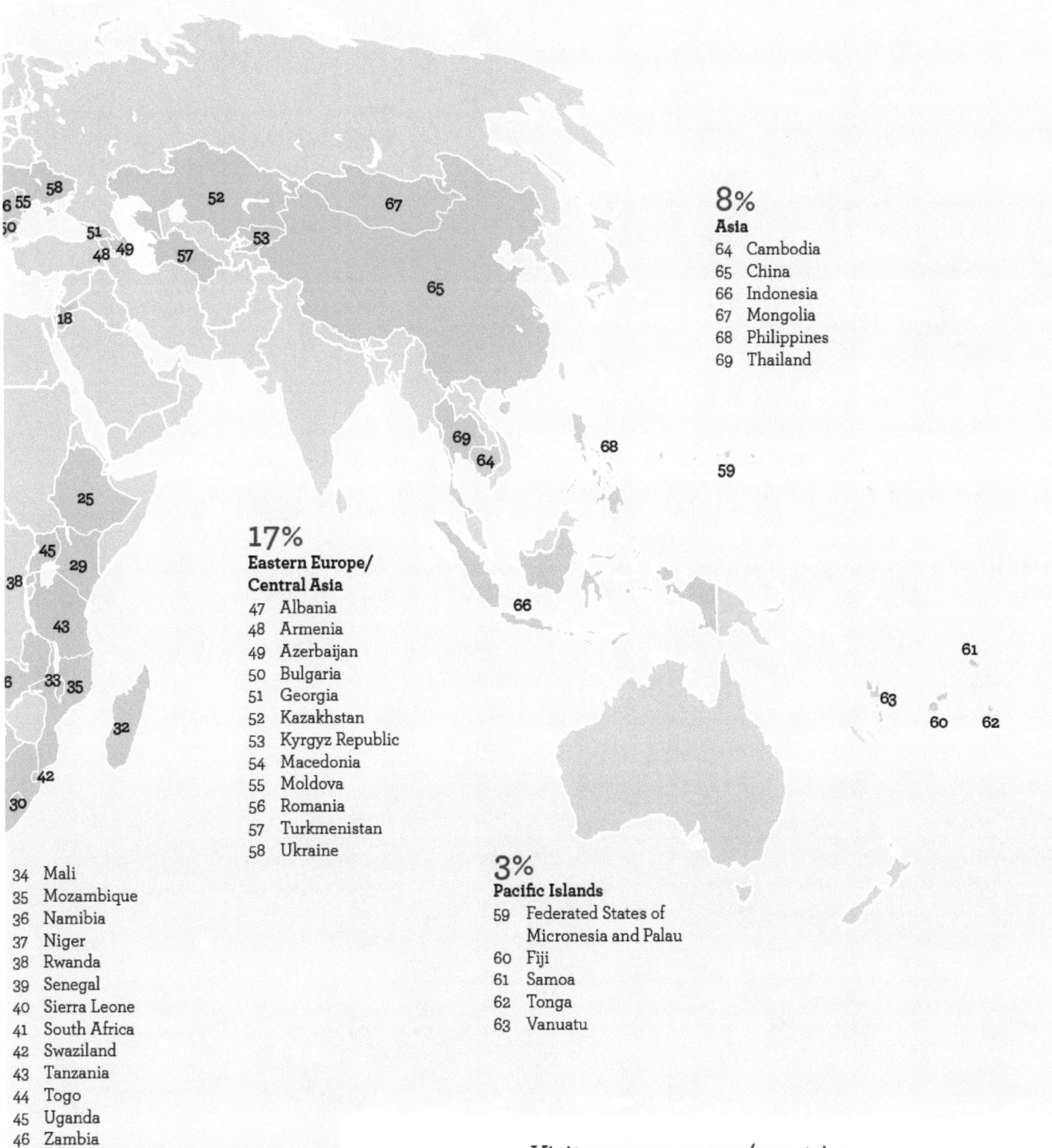

8%
Asia
64 Cambodia
65 China
66 Indonesia
67 Mongolia
68 Philippines
69 Thailand

17%
**Eastern Europe/
Central Asia**
47 Albania
48 Armenia
49 Azerbaijan
50 Bulgaria
51 Georgia
52 Kazakhstan
53 Kyrgyz Republic
54 Macedonia
55 Moldova
56 Romania
57 Turkmenistan
58 Ukraine

3%
Pacific Islands
59 Federated States of
    Micronesia and Palau
60 Fiji
61 Samoa
62 Tonga
63 Vanuatu

34 Mali
35 Mozambique
36 Namibia
37 Niger
38 Rwanda
39 Senegal
40 Sierra Leone
41 South Africa
42 Swaziland
43 Tanzania
44 Togo
45 Uganda
46 Zambia

*Visit peacecorps.gov/countries
for up-to-date information.*

Volunteer Work Areas

The type of work a Volunteer does is ultimately determined by the needs and priorities of a host country, the potential of a Volunteer to contribute to those priorities, and to Peace Corps' mission. There are a wide variety of Volunteer positions to fill throughout the world; however, nearly all Volunteers fall under one of the following general categories.

EDUCATION

This is the largest area of need for Peace Corps countries. Education Volunteers team-teach or directly teach English, health, literacy, math, and science. Education Volunteers strengthen local capacity by training and mentoring teachers in primary and secondary schools, teacher training colleges, and universities. Volunteers work with teachers to improve participatory teaching methodologies, inclusion practices, classroom management, authentic assessments, parental involvement, and gender equality in the classroom. They also create after-school programs, clubs, and camps for boys and girls to promote HIV/AIDS prevention and life skills.

A benefit of Volunteering as a teacher is that some states waive student teaching requirements or provide preliminary teaching credentials for returned Peace Corps Volunteers. All education positions require at least a bachelor's degree and a minimum GPA of 2.5.

YOUTH and COMMUNITY DEVELOPMENT

Volunteers work with youth to develop skills for transitioning from school to work, preparing for family life, and becoming engaged and active citizens in their communities. Volunteers also serve a valuable role in reaching special populations, such as orphans, street children, youth with disabilities, and other vulnerable young people. Volunteers build the capacity of the local people and organizations who work with youth.

HEALTH and HIV/AIDS

Health Volunteers work with local governments, clinics, nongovernmental organizations, and communities at the grassroots level, where the need is most urgent and the impact can be the greatest. They focus on outreach, social and behavior change in public health, maternal and child health, hygiene, water sanitation, and HIV/AIDS. Health Volunteers work in both formal and informal settings, targeting the groups most affected by a particular health issue.

Watch short videos about each work area at peacecorps.gov/workareas.

BUSINESS and INFORMATION & COMMUNICATION TECHNOLOGY

Business Volunteers work to build local capacity and improve economic opportunities in communities. They participate at many levels, whether helping artisan cooperatives to market their handmade goods, training entrepreneurs in basic small business skills development, or working with micro-finance institutions, nongovernmental organizations (NGOs) or municipalities to support local economic development projects.

Information and Communications Technology Volunteers help communities and organizations capitalize on available and appropriate information technology. Volunteers are also involved in computer teaching and training.

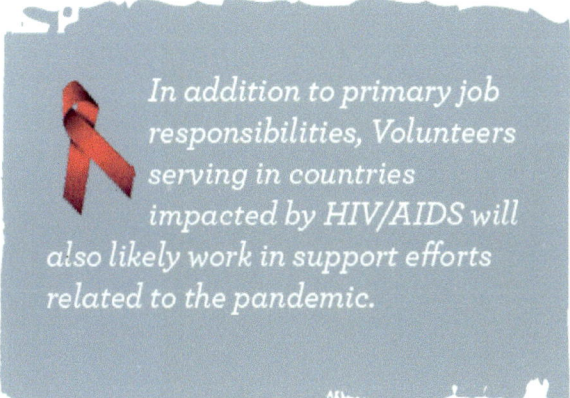

In addition to primary job responsibilities, Volunteers serving in countries impacted by HIV/AIDS will also likely work in support efforts related to the pandemic.

AGRICULTURE

Agriculture Volunteers work with small-scale farmers and families to increase food security and production and adapt to climate change while promoting environmental conservation practices. They introduce farmers to techniques that prevent soil erosion, reduce the use of harmful pesticides, and replenish the soil. They work alongside farmers on integrated projects that often combine vegetable gardening, livestock management, agroforestry, and food security. Agriculture Volunteers promote fruit and vegetable crops that provide valuable micronutrients, alleviating iodine, iron, and vitamin A deficiencies among children. They also help implement agribusiness programs to market and sell surplus food and cash crops.

ENVIRONMENT

Volunteers become leaders in grassroots efforts to protect and conserve the environment, engaging in projects that establish forest conservation plans and help promote alternative energy practices, integrate environmental curricula in schools, and promote alternative energy practices. They also collaborate with various organizations to promote environmental awareness activities such as wastewater management, recycling, environmental youth clubs, and park management. Volunteers strengthen communities' understanding of environmental issues, providing people with the knowledge to develop their own programs and make their own choices about how best to protect and conserve the local environment and adapt to climate change.

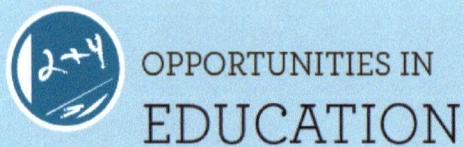

Secondary Education English Teaching

Overview

Volunteers teach English as a foreign language (TEFL), conversational English, or content-based English in middle and high schools. Volunteers:
- Share resources and develop teaching materials with local teachers through co-teaching and co-planning
- Become involved in community- and school-based projects
- Increase local students' English language competency and conversational skills
- Work in after-school programs, youth clubs, and library development

Education

Applicants may qualify with a bachelor's degree in any discipline and supplemental experience (described in the next column). Competitive applicants have a bachelor's degree in English, TEFL, or linguistics; **OR** state certification and supplemental experience.

Experience

Applicants must have at least three months or 30 hours of English, TEFL, foreign language, or literacy tutoring experience with middle school, high school, or adult students in classrooms or small group settings. Applicants can be recent college graduates or those with years of classroom experience. Other relevant experience includes community organizing and work with community groups; drama activities; health or HIV/AIDS education; civics education; youth development work, such as youth group counseling; and computer literacy.

Primary Education Teacher Training

Overview

Volunteers provide formal and informal training and support to elementary school teachers and provide classroom instruction. Volunteers:
- Work in one or several schools or teachers' colleges, modeling participatory methodologies, conducting workshops, and providing ongoing support to local teachers
- Develop primary education projects focusing specifically on the environment, early childhood development or special education, TEFL, literacy and math, science, or basic health education
- Co-teach or offer direct instruction to students

Education

Applicants must have a strong background in elementary education and a bachelor's degree in elementary or early childhood education; **OR** a bachelor's degree in any discipline and certification in elementary education; **OR** a bachelor's degree in any discipline and full-time classroom teaching experience at the preschool or elementary level for one year or more. Competitive applicants have state teaching certification.

Experience

Virtually all applicants have teaching experience, ranging from one semester of student teaching to many years of full-time teaching. Other relevant experience includes knowledge of teaching methodologies at the K–6 level, experience in development of educational materials, and skills in classroom management.

Secondary Education Math and Science Teaching

Overview

Volunteers in math teach basic concepts, including remedial math, geometry, algebra, statistics, probability, and calculus. Volunteers in science teach general science, biology, chemistry, and physics. Volunteers:
- Collaborate with local teachers to develop teaching materials and improve teaching techniques
- Integrate health and environmental education into the curriculum, and support other school and community activities, such as HIV/AIDS prevention and education

Education

Math: Applicants can qualify with a bachelor's degree in math, computer science, or engineering; **OR** a degree in any discipline with a minor in math (15 semester or 22 quarter hours); **OR** a degree in secondary education with a concentration in math; **OR** a degree in any discipline with certification in secondary math.

Science: Applicants can qualify with a bachelor's degree in general science, biology, chemistry, engineering, physics, or any physical or biological science; **OR** a degree in secondary education with a concentration in any science; **OR** a degree in any discipline with certification in secondary science; **OR** a degree in any discipline with a minor (15 semester or 22 quarter hours) in biology, chemistry, or physics.

Experience

Applicants typically have at least three months of experience in tutoring or informal teaching with small groups. Classroom teaching experience is preferred. Other relevant experience includes community service, especially with youth; youth development work; camp counseling; health and HIV/AIDS; environmental education; and computer literacy.

Secondary Education English Teacher Training

Overview

Volunteers train English teachers via formal classes, workshops, and informal activities. Volunteers:
- Work with new and experienced English teachers, train student teachers at teachers' colleges, or provide experienced teachers with in-service training in communicative methodologies, subject content, and resource development
- Increase local teachers' English language competency and conversational skills
- Encourage peer support and mentoring in their community

Education

Applicants must have a bachelor's degree in secondary education with a concentration in English, TEFL, or a foreign language; **OR** a bachelor's degree in these subjects and six months of full-time classroom teaching the same subjects at the secondary level; **OR** a bachelor's degree in any discipline and full-time classroom teaching experience in the same subjects at the secondary level for one year or more; **OR** a bachelor's degree in any discipline with secondary education state certification in English, TEFL, or a foreign language; **OR** a master's degree in education with a concentration in English, TEFL, or a foreign language; **OR** a master's degree in teaching English, TEFL, a foreign language, or applied linguistics.

Experience

All applicants are university graduates with experience as student teachers, graduate teaching assistants, or substitute teachers; or they have at least six months of full-time teaching experience. Applicants should be comfortable working in large classroom settings.

Special Education Teacher Training

Overview

Volunteers work with education offices, schools, and local teachers of students with special needs. Volunteers:
- Focus on methodology, individualized instruction, classroom management, and resource development for teachers
- Work with parents and communities to develop projects to raise public awareness and understanding of people with disabilities

Education

Applicants must have a bachelor's degree in special education; **OR** a bachelor's degree with certification in special education; **OR** a bachelor's degree in education with one year full-time experience working with populations described in the next column; **OR** a bachelor's degree in any discipline with one year of experience described in the next column.

Experience

Applicants must have experience working with those who have learning or developmental disabilities; emotional, physical, or multiple handicaps; or those who are hearing or visually impaired. This experience can range from student teaching to many years of teaching in a school system or working in an institution. Many applicants have experience working with individuals with disabilities in group homes or other organizations.

University English Teaching

Overview

Volunteers provide formal and informal training, instruction, and support to students and faculty. Volunteers:
- Help students make use of academic and technical resources published in English in their study of languages, literature, business, or other fields
- Teach English grammar, conversation, phonetics, American literature and culture, creative writing, and linguistics
- Establish English language clubs and resource centers
- Share ideas and develop materials with fellow teachers
- Integrate communicative teaching techniques into the classroom

Education

Applicants must have a master's degree in English or any foreign language; **OR** a master's degree in TEFL or linguistics. Some applicants with supplemental experience may qualify with a master's degree in English, history, language arts, humanities, or other social science with supplemental experience.

Experience

Most applicants have full- or part-time experience as graduate teaching assistants, substitute teachers, tutors, or student teachers. Other relevant experience includes working with community organizations or on projects involving adult literacy programs, environmental or health education, or drama activities; and editing or writing for college literary magazines or newspapers.

Community Development

Overview

Volunteers act as catalysts for change by working within their communities on projects in many Peace Corps work areas. Volunteers:

- Focus on community development projects in education, youth development, health and HIV/AIDS, environment, and business development
- Conduct community outreach and needs assessments

Education

Applicants can qualify with a bachelor's degree in social work, counseling, or community development; **OR** a bachelor's degree in any discipline, along with significant volunteer experience in education, youth development, health and HIV/AIDS, the environment, and/or business.

Experience

Applicants must demonstrate experience in planning, organizing, counseling, or leadership within the past five years. This experience may be in education, youth development, health and HIV/ AIDS, the environment, and/or business. Other relevant experience includes knowledge of adult education and teaching methodology, conducting needs assessments, and a leadership position in a club or organization.

Youth Development

Overview

Volunteers work with at-risk youth ages 10 to 25, helping communities develop programs to assist young people. Volunteers:

- Support the development of life skills through healthy lifestyles training, including HIV/AIDS awareness, reproductive health, and nutrition
- Prepare youth for the world of work through financial literacy, employability skills, and career planning
- Engage youth as active citizens through service learning and civic involvement
- Work with parents, teachers, and community organizations to support youth development

Education

Applicants must have an associate degree and one year of full-time counseling experience with at-risk youth; **OR** five years of relevant full-time work experience; **OR** a bachelor's degree in any discipline with six consecutive months of full-time experience; **OR** a master's of social work; **OR** be a licensed social worker with youth experience. All experience must be relevant, as described in the next column.

Experience

Applicants must have at least six months of full-time work experience teaching or counseling in at-risk youth programs. Other qualifying experience includes full-time work in one or more of the following categories: youth; conflict resolution or mediation skills; HIV/AIDS counseling or awareness training; coaching or working with physically or mentally disabled youth; or with national and community service programs.

HEALTH and HIV/AIDS

Health Extension

Overview

Volunteers carry out social and behavior change activities for improved public health, while enhancing the capacity of community partners and service providers. Volunteers:
- Build the capacity of health providers in participatory and inter-personal communication for improved maternal and child health
- Promote social and behavior change through the creation and/or strengthening of peer groups (e.g. women's groups, youth groups) and through sports and recreational activities
- Educate students and youth about healthy lifestyles and life skills
- Enhance the organizational capacity of partners providing health services
- Build the capacity of community partners to organize and conduct social behavior change events, such as radio, theatre, puppet shows, and health-themed activities

Education

Applicants must have a bachelor's degree in any discipline and a demonstrated interest in community health; **OR** be a registered nurse with a demonstrated interest in community health.

Experience

Interest in health is demonstrated through volunteer or work experience in areas such as HIV/AIDS outreach, hospice, family planning counseling, emergency medical technician (EMT) or CPR certification, and hands-on care giving in a hospital, clinic, or lab technician setting. Counseling or teaching in health subjects may also qualify as experience for this program.

Public Health Education

Overview

Volunteers promote behavior and organizational change, including health systems planning and coordination by working with organizations and/or with ministries of health at the district, regional, and national levels. Volunteers:
- Improve the capacity of health providers to carry out strategic planning and manage information systems
- Strengthen linkages between health facilities, organizations, and communities
- Build the capacity of community partners to organize and conduct social behavior change events, such as radio, theatre, puppet shows, and health-themed activities
- Support the strengthening of organizations providing health services

Education

Applicants must have a bachelor's degree in health education, nutrition, or dietetics; **OR** a master's degree in public health; **OR** be a registered nurse certified in public health or midwifery; **OR** be a certified physician's assistant.

Experience

Competitive applicants have been active, on a volunteer basis, in health-related activities in colleges or their communities, working, for example, as peer nutritionists, HIV/AIDS or sexually transmitted infections counselors, or resident advisors in dormitories. Many are pre-med students who have shadowed doctors in hospitals. Other relevant skills include expertise in disease surveillance, creative training and adult education techniques, behavior change, and community entry and survey methods.

Water and Sanitation Extension

Overview

Volunteers work on construction projects and help organize and mobilize communities to provide health and hygiene education. Volunteers:
- Tap springs, construct wells, and build latrines
- Improve or construct potable water storage and distribution facilities
- Conduct community outreach to heighten awareness of water, sanitation, health, and environment issues
- Strengthen technical and management capabilities of local water communities

Education

Applicants can qualify with a bachelor's degree in any discipline; **OR** one year of full-time construction experience.

Experience

Applicants with a degree usually have at least three months of experience in a relevant area or hands-on experience in mechanical repairs, construction, carpentry, or set design.

Applicants without a degree should have at least one year of work experience in construction, masonry, carpentry, or plumbing. Competitive applicants will have three to five years experience as mentioned above.

All applicants should have excellent physical stamina and be interested in hands-on work.

Environmental and Water Resources Engineering

Overview

Volunteers work with local governments and communities to improve water and sanitation facilities. Volunteers:
- Train people in facilities operation and maintenance
- Help communities access resources and form or strengthen local water or solid waste committees to sustain facilities
- Design and build potable water sources, sewage, and irrigation systems
- Design and build solid waste management systems and structures, earthen dams, and concrete spillways
- Conduct community outreach to heighten awareness of water, sanitation, health, and environmental issues

Education

Applicants can qualify with a bachelor's or master's degree in environmental or sanitary engineering; **OR** a bachelor's or master's degree in civil engineering with 12 semester hours of environmental engineering course work; **OR** certification in water or wastewater treatment plant operation or hazardous materials management.

Experience

Relevant experience or demonstrated interest includes mechanics or construction, hydrology, community outreach in health or environmental awareness, and simple accounting and budgeting. Applicants also should have excellent physical stamina.

Note: Most of these positions require Spanish language.

Construction and Skilled Trades

Overview

Volunteers work with communities and local governments to facilitate the construction of potable water, sanitation, and irrigation infrastructures. Volunteers:

- Transfer construction skills to tradespeople and students in their communities
- Estimate costs and quantities of materials, determine types of tools required, assure inventory control, work with industrial equipment, and teach building techniques
- Teach vocational education in schools, technical institutes, and training centers
- Conduct community outreach to heighten awareness of water, sanitation, health, and environmental issues

Education

Applicants must have a bachelor's degree in industrial arts, technical education, or any other discipline and at least six months of work experience; **OR** two or more years of full-time journeyman work experience as described in the next column.

Experience

Relevant experience includes journeyman work in general construction, masonry, carpentry, or plumbing. Other relevant skills include proven leadership experience in youth or adult service organizations, demonstrated interest in teaching or tutoring, and community organizing or outreach. All applicants should be eager to work with their hands and transfer their skills to others.

Note: Most of these positions require Spanish language.

BUSINESS ᴀɴᴅ INFORMATION & COMMUNICATION TECHNOLOGY

Business Advising

Overview

Volunteers work in a variety of settings assisting businesses and public institutions, local and regional governments, nonprofit organizations, women's educational institutions and youth groups, artisans, and other aspiring business owners. Volunteers:
- Teach business courses and business English, and facilitate business training workshops
- Train and advise entrepreneurs and managers in business planning, marketing, financial management, and product design
- Advise agricultural cooperatives, agribusinesses, and farmers
- Develop fundraising plans and write project funding proposals
- Work with business service providers
- Work with artisans and entrepreneurs to improve business practices, marketing techniques, and sales
- Help develop the local community-based tourism industry

Education

Applicants must have a bachelor's degree in business, economics, management, finance, marketing, accounting, computer systems, or international business; **OR** a degree in any discipline with one year full-time experience in cooperatives, bookkeeping, small business, or credit unions; **OR** four or more years of business management experience; **OR** an associate degree in any business discipline with two years of experience as a business manager.

Experience

Most applicants have worked for at least one year in small business management, accounting, microfinance, or with cooperatives. Other relevant experience includes management in a multiple-task environment, owning or operating a small business, and volunteer work with community- or school-based organizations or clubs. Some applicants also have experience in human resource development or training, market research and financial advising, and fundraising. Project management experience, information technology skills, and agribusiness experience are also useful.

Nongovernmental Organization Development

Overview

Volunteers work with local, national, or international governmental organizations, or nongovernmental organizations (NGOs) that focus on youth, social services, health services, HIV/AIDS prevention, small business development, or the environment. Volunteers:
- Increase an NGO's organizational capacity and sustainability
- Create annual strategic and funding plans
- Raise public awareness of an NGO's mission and conduct community outreach
- Recruit, train, and motivate NGO volunteers
- Develop mission statements, bylaws, organizational charts, job descriptions, and other documentation for good governance
- Develop fundraising programs and provide assistance with grant writing, transparency, and accountability
- Work with boards of directors and staff to mentor and build management skills
- Increase the quality and effectiveness of an NGO's services

Education

Applicants must have a bachelor's degree in any discipline and two years of full-time experience in management of a nonprofit; **OR** a master's degree with a concentration in nonprofit management, public administration, or organizational development; **OR** five years of management experience in a nonprofit organization.

Experience

Most applicants have at least two years of management or organizational development experience with nonprofit organizations as staff members or volunteers serving in a leadership role. Recent college graduates may have experience as founders or leaders of a community- or school-based organization. Other relevant experience includes a demonstrated commitment to a project's issues, working with a community service organization, and supervision of community or student volunteers. Networking skills, a law degree with NGO or board of director experience, information technology skills, and strategic planning abilities are also useful.

Business Development

Overview

Volunteers work on projects in community agencies, educational institutions, financial institutions, chambers of commerce, tourism centers, cooperatives, farmers' associations, or other economic development organizations. Volunteers:

- Advise businesses and conduct seminars on starting a business, strategic planning, marketing, merchandising, organizational development, and tourism development
- Teach basic business skills, business English, and financial education to women, youth, and minority groups to strengthen their participation in the economic system
- Assist local and regional governments in planning and implementing economic development strategies
- Train and advise entrepreneurs and managers in business planning, marketing, financial management, and product design

Education

Applicants must have a master's degree in business administration, public administration, management, accounting, banking, or finance; **OR** a bachelor's degree in business administration, management, accounting, banking, public administration, or finance and two years of full-time business work experience; **OR** a bachelor's degree in any discipline and five years of full-time business work experience.

Experience

Most applicants have at least two years of business experience in accounting, finance, management, or marketing. Many have experience starting and running their own businesses. Other relevant experience includes knowledge of various management practices, computer skills, financial management or budget experience, and significant hands-on entrepreneurial or business experience.

Note: Approximately half of these positions require a Romance language background.

Information & Communication Technology

Overview

Volunteers provide technical training and support to school systems, health ministries, municipal government offices, and nongovernmental organizations. Volunteers:

- Teach computer skills and data processing
- Help bring the Internet into classrooms and provide forums for communities to share ideas about development activities
- Help develop regional databases and implement networks for businesses and government offices to allow the linking of entrepreneurs to new business opportunities
- Expand farmers' access to information on market prices
- Facilitate the creation, storage, management, and dissemination of information by electronic means, including computer, Internet, radio, and video

Education

Applicants can qualify with a bachelor's degree in computer science or information systems; **OR** a bachelor's degree in any discipline with 15 semester or 22 quarter hours in computer science and two years of related experience; **OR** a bachelor's degree with a focus on communication technologies, including mass communications, graphic design, informatics, and telecommunications; **OR** five or more years of experience in programming, systems analysis, systems design, or computer consulting; **OR** an associate degree in a computer-related field and two years of computer experience.

Experience

Applicants must have knowledge of, or experience in, basic computer applications, such as word processing, spreadsheets, and databases, and have strong leadership and organizational skills. Other relevant experience includes an ability to train others in computer literacy, computer maintenance, and repair skills; development of training materials; and experience in Web-based technology such as HTML, website design, or online marketing.

Agriculture and Forestry Extension

Overview

Volunteers work on a variety of production and conservation projects. Volunteers:

- Establish and maintain soil and water conservation structures and practices
- Raise trees in small nurseries and work in fruit tree production, live fences, and other agriculture-related forestry practices
- Collaborate with individual farmers and associations to improve agriculture and agribusiness practices
- Train communities in nutritional education through vegetable gardening and permaculture in rural or urban areas
- Help with income generation activities such as aquaculture, value-added product development, apiculture, and small animal husbandry

Education

Applicants can qualify with a bachelor's degree in any discipline and a minimum of three months full-time experience described in the next column; **OR** one year of full-time experience described in the next column.

Experience

Applicants with a degree must have three months of full-time experience with a large-scale commercial or family-run business involving vegetable gardening, farming, nursery work, tree planting or care, urban forestry, livestock (dairy or beef cattle, pigs, sheep, or chickens) care or management, or fish (freshwater or marine) cultivation or production. Other relevant experience that is helpful includes an interest and background in environmental issues and formal or informal teaching or tutoring of adults and/or youth, or interest or experience in income generating agriculture activities.

Applicants without a degree must have one year full-time hands-on experience such as vegetable gardening, nursery work, tree planting, or urban forestry. Competitive applicants will have 3–5 years of such experience.

Applied Agricultural Sciences

Overview

Volunteers encourage sustainable crop production by working hand-in-hand with farmers to introduce organic farming techniques, better farm management, and promote development of small agriculture business projects. Volunteers:

- Conduct workshops on integrated pest management
- Introduce composting, green manures, and other soil-improvement techniques
- Test new varieties of seeds and demonstrate post-harvest management methods
- Teach agriculture and extension methodologies in formal training institutions
- Develop marketing strategies

Education

Applicants must have a bachelor's or associate degree in agronomy or horticulture; **OR** three years of full-time farm experience; **OR** a bachelor's degree in any discipline plus 18 months full-time farming experience; **OR** a bachelor's degree in botany or entomology plus six months of fruit or vegetable growing experience; **OR** a bachelor's degree in biology with substantial coursework in agricultural science, botany, or entomology plus six months of fruit or vegetable growing experience.

Experience

Competitive applicants have a solid background in agricultural production on family or commercial farms. They have grown fruits and vegetables and understand concepts such as soil fertility and integrated pest management. Other relevant experience includes interest in, and knowledge of, organic farming, mechanical skills from using farm machinery, some experience with livestock, and knowledge of food storage and preservation.

Farm Management and Agribusiness

Overview

Volunteers work with small-scale farmers, farmers' cooperatives, agribusinesses, and nongovernmental organizations. Volunteers:

- Teach basic business practices such as marketing, credit price determination, and general business planning
- Work on crop and livestock production and preservation
- Assist in organizing networks of local farmers
- Identify market structures and channels
- Perform production cost and price analysis

Education

Applicants can qualify with a bachelor's degree in agriculture economics or agribusiness; **OR** a degree that combines agriculture and management; **OR** a business or economics degree combined with one year of hands-on experience in farming or agribusiness; **OR** at least three years of full-time experience in farm management or agribusiness.

Experience

Competitive applicants have hands-on work experience in agriculture management or farming as well as general knowledge of business and marketing concepts.

Environmental Education and Awareness

Overview

Volunteers help communities manage their natural resources and promote environmental education. Volunteers:
- Teach in elementary and secondary schools and provide environmental education to youth groups and individuals outside school settings
- Oversee organizational development of environmental groups
- Promote sustainable use of land- or marine-based resources
- Develop and promote community-based ecotourism and other income-generating activities for communities living near protected areas
- Teach soil conservation, forestry, and vegetable gardening practices

Education

Applicants can qualify with a bachelor's degree in an environmental field such as environmental science, ecology, or natural resource conservation; OR a degree in any discipline with two years of professional experience organizing or leading environmental activities. Most applicants have significant course work in science.

Experience

Most applicants have six months experience in related internships or study-abroad programs. Many have had seasonal employment educating the public on environmental issues. Other relevant experience includes conducting biological surveys of plants or animals, initiating environmental campaigns, planting trees or conducting other conservation activities, and grant writing for conservation efforts.

Forestry

Overview

Volunteers help communities with projects to conserve natural resources. Volunteers:
- Conduct soil conservation and reforestation projects
- Oversee watershed management and flood control
- Encourage production of sustainable fuels
- Improve agroforestry practices, such as fruit production
- Build live fences and alley cropping
- Encourage preservation of biodiversity, sometimes near national parks or other reserves
- Utilize GIS/GPS in land use planning

Education

Applicants can qualify with a bachelor's or associate degree in forestry, watershed or natural resource management, environmental science, or ecology; OR a degree in biology, botany, or geology and six months of growing or field experience; OR a degree in any discipline and three years of work experience in forestry or nursery management.

Experience

Most applicants have at least six months of practical experience in gardening, farming, or nursery management. Other relevant experience includes vegetable production using organic and low-input methods, tree planting or other conservation activities, landscaping, a high level of comfort working outdoors, an understanding of how natural resources can be managed to sustain people's livelihoods, and use of computer applications such as geographic information systems for environmental research and modeling.

Protected Area Management

Overview

Volunteers provide technical assistance and training in natural resource conservation, generally in close affiliation with national parks or other reserves. Volunteers:

- Provide technical training to park managers, guards, and guides
- Promote community-based conservation, such as sustainable use of land- or marine-based resources
- Promote ecotourism and other income-generating activities for communities living near protected areas

Education

Applicants can qualify with a bachelor's degree in wildlife biology, wildlife management, natural resource management, or park administration; **OR** a degree in any discipline and three years of work experience in park planning or administration, resource management, or wildlife management.

Experience

Most applicants have experience in providing technical assistance and training in natural resource management through volunteer work or internships. Other relevant experience includes conducting biological surveys of plants or animals, initiating environmental campaigns, tree planting or other local conservation activities, and grant writing for conservation efforts.

"As a Peace Corps Volunteer I saw how interconnected we all are, and how helping one helps many."

Dorothy Sales
Volunteer in Ukraine

"Some people say their Peace Corps experience launched their career. For me, it ignited my passion for building companies that address the needs of disenfranchised populations. I can't calculate the opportunity cost of discovering my passion; to me it's invaluable."

Brian Forde
Volunteer in Nicaragua

"Being a Peace Corps Volunteer has allowed me to put my degree to good use, travel and explore the culture and lifestyle of people outside the United States, and learn more about myself."

Jessica Blatt
Volunteer in Paraguay

"My Peace Corps experience really enhanced my interest in agriculture and led me to work at the U.S. Department of Agriculture. I used the noncompetitive eligibility benefit when I applied for my position. Bringing that world view to my job makes me more effective because I've got a broader perspective than most, and I owe that to the Peace Corps."

Caitrin Martin
Volunteer in Senegal

The Peace Corps offers a unique experience to make a difference around the world and bring the benefits of that experience back home. The personal and professional rewards of Peace Corps service last a lifetime.

Tear out this page
to use as your
personal reference

Application Process Tipsheet & Checklist

Prior to Applying

- Research all the information you need to make an informed decision about committing to the Peace Corps
- Review the list of medical conditions that the Peace Corps is typically unable to support at **peacecorps.gov/medical**
- Attend an in-person or online information session to learn more about the opportunities and realities of service. Talk with returned Peace Corps Volunteers. See **peacecorps.gov/events**
- Speak to a recruiter by calling **800.424.8580**

Submitting Your Application

- Begin the application process by going to **peacecorps.gov/apply**
- Prepare the following information:
  - ☐ Three references and contact information— work supervisor, volunteer supervisor, personal (the person cannot be related to you)
  - ☐ Your employment, volunteer history, and practical skills experience
  - ☐ Your resume
  - ☐ Two essays demonstrating your motivation and cross-cultural experience. Each essay should be between 250-500 words
  - ☐ College transcripts unless, generally, you have 10 years applicable professional experience (an unofficial copy is acceptable)
  - ☐ Outline of outstanding student loan(s), credit card(s), mortgage, or other financial obligations
    - If someone else will assume responsibility for financial obligations during your Peace Corps service, a notarized letter is required from him or her stating this
    - If you have financial obligations, provide us with a narrative regarding the obligations and your plan to satisfy them while overseas
  - ☐ If you are married and applying to serve without your spouse, get a notarized letter from your spouse stating his or her support
  - ☐ Store your application password for later

☐ Proofread your application, essays, and resume before final submission

☐ Complete and submit the application

☐ Complete and submit the Health History Form

Application Follow-up

After you submit your application, you should hear from your recruitment office within two weeks.

If you are considering the graduate school program, Masters International, apply to the school first and then apply to the Peace Corps. Get more information at **peacecorps.gov/masters.**

Peace Corps Application Quick Reference

My recruiter's name and phone number:

_____

_____

_____

My candidate reference # is: _____

My email login is: _____

My password is: _____

After Nomination

My recruiter nominated me on this date:

_____

The tentative region of my assignment is:

_____

My estimated departure date is:

_____

☐ **Remember to complete your fingerprint cards and National Agency Checklist form and mail them back to the Peace Corps as soon as possible.**

*All of the above **may change** between nomination and invitation! Fill in these blanks yourself as you receive information from the Peace Corps.*

Medical Qualification

Expect email correspondence from the medical office within 48 hours of nomination. If you haven't received contact via email after a week, contact your recruiter.

All requests will be accompanied by specific instructions on what medical information is required. Make sure you follow all of the instructions exactly,

For more information, talk to a Peace Corps recruiter at 800.424.8580, and visit peacecorps.gov.

as errors will delay processing. The best way to return information is to scan and upload documentation to the medical team. You may fax or mail in documents, but please be aware that faxing or mailing documents may delay receipt for up to four weeks. Always remember to keep a photocopy of everything. It is important to submit all medical forms as soon as possible. If you anticipate a delay, please contact your evaluation nurse or assistant for advice.

Legal Clearance

If there are any legal issues identified by the Legal Office, you might be asked to provide additional information.

Placement

Only contact the Placement Office after you have been legally cleared. If you do not hear from your placement officer and your departure month is less than four months away, contact your recruiter for your placement officer's phone number.

My placement officer is:

_____

He or she can be reached at this number:

_____

Invitation

The Placement Office will review your file once you are legally cleared.

Invitations are determined by a number of factors, including medical support (if any), program availability, and applicant suitability. Flexibility is key.

If invited, my letter will indicate a deadline to respond. My deadline is: _____

Take the next step

and explore how the Peace Corps can fit into your future.

View extensive resources
peacecorps.gov

Speak with your local recruiter
800.424.8580

Attend an informational meeting
near you or online
peacecorps.gov/events

Begin your application
online today!
peacecorps.gov/apply

Peace Corps Recruitment Offices

Atlanta Region

(AL, FL, GA, MS, PR, SC, TN, USVI)
60 Forsyth Street
Suite 3M40
Atlanta, GA 30303
P: 404.562.3456
F: 404.562.3455
atlinfo@peacecorps.gov

Chicago Region

(IA, IL, IN, KY, MI, MN, MO, ND, OH, SD, WI)
55 West Monroe Street
Suite 450
Chicago, IL 60603
P: 312.353.4990
F: 312.353.4192
chicago@peacecorps.gov

Dallas Region

(AR, CO, KS, LA, NE, NM, OK, TX, UT, WY)
1100 Commerce Street
Suite 427
Dallas, TX 75242
P: 214.253.5400
F: 214.253.5401
dallas@peacecorps.gov

Headquarters

Peace Corps
Paul D. Coverdell
Peace Corps Headquarters
1111 20th Street, NW
Washington, DC 20526
P: 800.424.8580

Los Angeles Region

(AZ, Southern CA)
2361 Rosecrans Avenue
Suite 155
El Segundo, CA 90245
P: 310.356.1100
F: 310.356.1125
lainfo@peacecorps.gov

Mid-Atlantic Region

(DC, DE, MD, NC, VA, WV)
Attn: Recruitment Office
1111 20th Street, NW
Washington, DC 20526
P: 202.692.1040
F: 202.692.1065
dcinfo@peacecorps.gov

Northeast Region

(CT, MA, ME, NH, NJ, NY, PA, RI, VT)
201 Varick Street
Suite 1025
New York, NY 10014
P: 212.352.5440
F: 212.352.5441
nyinfo@peacecorps.gov

San Francisco Region

(Northern CA, HI, NV)
1301 Clay Street
Suite 620N
Oakland, CA 94612
P: 510.452.8444
F: 510.452.8441
sfinfo@peacecorps.gov

Seattle Region

(AK, ID, MT, OR, WA)
1601 Fifth Avenue
Suite 605
Seattle, WA 98101
P: 206.553.5490
F: 206.553.2343
seattle@peacecorps.gov

For more information, talk to a Peace Corps recruiter at **800.424.8580,** *and visit* **peacecorps.gov**

Friend us, fan us, follow us:

Facebook: facebook.com/peacecorps
Twitter: twitter.com/peacecorps
YouTube: youtube.com/peacecorps
Flickr: flickr.com/peacecorps
Tumblr: peacecorps.tumblr.com
LinkedIn: linkedin.com/company/peace-corps
Peace Corps Digital Library: peacecorps.gov/collection

Learn about Peace Corps in under 13 minutes! Watch the film short at **peacecorps.gov/be**

www.ingramcontent.com/pod-product-compliance
Lightning Source LLC
Chambersburg PA
CBHW041521280526

45792CB00004B/1337